comix

THE PLANET MACHINE

Steve Bowkett

Illustrated by Liz McIntosh

Read about my brilliant plan to destroy Earth for good!

comix

1 **Joker** · Anthony Masters
2 **Sam's Dream** · Michael Hardcastle
3 **Arf and the Greedy Grabber** · Philip Wooderson
4 **Jack's Tree** · Georgia Byng
5 **The Planet Machine** · Steve Bowkett
6 **Mr Potts the Potty Teacher** · Colin West

First paperback edition 2001
First published 2000 in hardback by
A & C Black (Publishers) Ltd
35 Bedford Row, London WC1R 4JH

Text copyright © 2000 Steve Bowkett
Illustrations copyright © 2000 Liz McIntosh

ISBN 0-7136-5404-X

A CIP catalogue for this book is available from the
British Library.

Printed and bound in Spain by G. Z. Printek, Bilbao

CHAPTER ONE

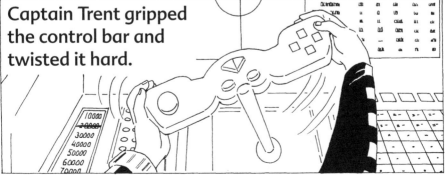

Captain Trent gripped the control bar and twisted it hard.

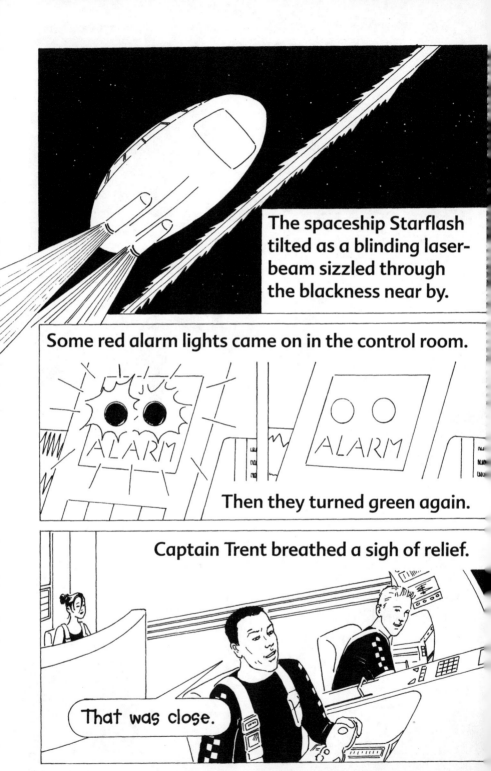

The spaceship Starflash tilted as a blinding laser-beam sizzled through the blackness near by.

Some red alarm lights came on in the control room.

Then they turned green again.

Captain Trent breathed a sigh of relief.

That was close.

Benny Rigel was in charge of the engines. He stared at his monitor screens, then smiled.

Any problems with the ship?

How are the computers, Wu?

No problems with the stardrive, Captain. We'll catch those criminals yet!

Maybe.

5

Wu Li was the third member of the crew. She knew more about computers than anyone else alive.

There are no problems, Captain.

The flight path of the White Lightning will take it into the Asteroid Belt in fifteen minutes.

Trent nodded grimly. White Lightning was the spaceship used by the Quicksilver Gang to commit their crimes. All the Space Cops in the Solar System had been after the gang for months.

Captain Trent rubbed his chin.

If White Lightning reaches the asteroids, it will be very difficult to track. We might lose sight of it completely.

The gang is bound to hide out in the Belt.

Mr Sleek and his crew could land on any big rock and we'd never find them then!

So we must catch them now!

Captain Trent used the control bar again and sent Starflash streaking through space towards the dangers of the Asteroid Belt.

This is a zone of rocks orbiting between Mars and Jupiter. Some asteroids are many miles across, while others are no bigger than pebbles. But even the smallest could destroy a spaceship moving at star-speed.

Even so, the Captain had confidence in the skill and bravery of his crew.

And besides, it was time that Mr Sleek — leader of the Quicksilver Gang — paid for his crimes.

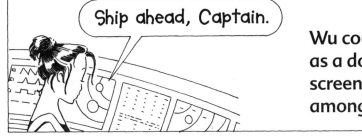

Ship ahead, Captain.

Wu could see it as a dot on her screen, drifting among the stars.

And she's firing on us again!

Her voice lifted in alarm.

Trent saw the glitter of lasers and sent Starflash diving behind a mountainous asteroid.

The high-power beams struck the asteroid and it exploded into a shower of stones.

The crew heard them banging on the hull.

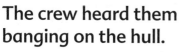

The force screens won't take it.

Any more like that, Captain, and we're done for.

Trent thought hard for a moment.

Okay... Wu, Benny, we'll try a final approach. If we can cripple Mr Sleek's ship and knock out the engines, we can board her.

Whatever you say, Captain.

Benny grinned. He was already busy at his controls.

Wu Li was frowning.

Wu?

Um, yes sir, of course... But I'm getting some strange readings on my screens...

Captain Trent hardly heard her.

He flicked switches and pressed buttons.

Then he pushed the control bar and Starflash streaked forwards with a burst of dazzling fire.

CHAPTER TWO

Some distance away, on board the White Lightning, Mr Sleek was laughing. He had seen the asteroid explode near his enemies, the Space Cops.

Those fools! Don't they know the Quicksilver Gang can never be caught?

His crew, Tulley and Gron, were not so sure. The asteroids all around were beginning to look like a snowstorm.

Hey, Tulley, I'm getting strange readings on my screens...

'Don't bother me now,' Tulley snapped.

He looked around.

Mr Sleek, Starflash is moving towards us. Those cops haven't given up yet.

Then they're even stupider than I thought.

Mr Sleek's thin face twisted in anger.

Gron, is there an asteroid nearby big enough for us to land on?

'Aye sir,' Gron growled. 'There's a huge rock just ahead, but...'

Mr Sleek clenched his fists.

We'll put down there. Then, as the Starflash passes over, we'll channel all our fire-power into a single laser blast. I'm going to turn Captain Adam Trent into space dust!'

CHAPTER THREE

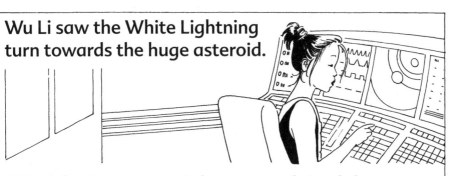

Wu Li saw the White Lightning turn towards the huge asteroid.

'We're losing contact,' she reported, 'and the strange readings are getting stranger!'

Captain Trent frowned.

Benny, take control for a while.

He left his seat and crossed the cabin to Wu Li.

Give me a picture on the main display.

Wu used her keyboard.

A glowing TV picture appeared above them.

Okay.

There's the asteroid... and that speck must be White Lightning.

'Look,' Trent pointed.

'Mr Sleek's taking his ship down to land.'

'If we lose him now, we'll never find him again.'

I don't like it, sir, Sleek isn't just going to wait for us to go away. They're bound to —

'Wait!' Captain Trent interrupted. He'd seen something on the screens. Something vast. Something terrible.

Look at that, Wu! Do you see it?

'C-Captain,' Wu stammered. 'It's — it's amazing — And it's moving straight towards White Lightning.'

CHAPTER FOUR

Mr Sleek stared at the asteroid below.

He had never seen such a dark and depressing place.

Massive craters and mighty valleys were sunk in shadow.

Pale sunlight gleamed on grey rocks...

Then, on the skyline, something glittered.

More than that, the thing was moving. But was it one object, or many?

For a few seconds, Mr Sleek wasn't sure.

Near by, Gron was still muttering about strange readings on the screen.

But this was far stranger. This was simply incredible.

Suddenly, all of the objects came together and lifted into space. Mr Sleek understood what he was seeing.

And he screamed.

CHAPTER FIVE

Captain Trent, Benny and Wu Li crowded around the monitor screen.

From behind the asteroid, a huge creature had appeared.

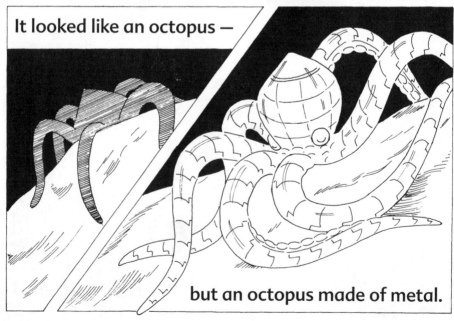

It looked like an octopus —

but an octopus made of metal.

Its many tentacles had been feeling along the valleys and craters.

But as White Lightning zoomed by, the thing had reached out towards it.

Now, the octopus-robot wrapped itself around Mr Sleek's spaceship.

Fire blazed from hidden jets in the monster's body.

It began moving faster and faster towards the curtain of light Wu Li had seen earlier.

Then both the octopus and its victim — vanished.

Nobody said a word for several minutes.

Benny rubbed his eyes, as though he'd been dreaming.

Wu Li looked at her shaking hands and tried to calm herself.

Captain Trent spoke at last.

Well, you don't see something like that every day!

Sir, this is crazy. What was that thing? Where's it gone?

Whatever it was, it was heading for that light.

And what's happened to the Quicksilver Gang?

They're on their way to the light too. I think it's a force field.

And whatever lies behind it will give us the answers we need.

Maybe it would be better to report back to Headquarters.

Except, we can't use the starlight radio because of interference from the force field...

And by the time we've returned to Mars Base, that robot-thing might have gone.

Benny gave a great sigh.

Captain Trent smiled brightly.

So. There's only one thing to do...

I don't want to hear it!

Wu, follow the robot to the force field.

As Starflash reached the weird curtain of light, it slowed down.

CHAPTER SIX

Trent eased the control bar forward.

His ship slid like a silver coin into the unknown.

Whatever's in there, it's huge. I'm getting gravity readings... We must be approaching a planet!

There are no planets in this part of space, the nearest world is Mars. That's millions of miles away.

But I'm telling you it's a planet!

Captain Trent could see she was frightened. They all were.

Just calm down.

I'll take the ship forward very slowly.

We can always turn back if we need to.

Soon afterwards, the shimmering light faded.

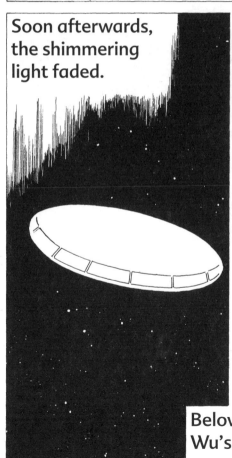

Below the ship, the surface of Wu's 'planet' came into view.

Towers and domes stretched as far as the eye could see.

And there were mountains too, and valleys and plains which, like the octopus-robot, were all made entirely of metal.

Somebody or something, has built this world.

But who?

Why?

'The shape of it reminds me of creatures from another star system I learnt about at the Academy. We'll talk about it later,' Wu Li gulped.

Right now, we're being attacked.

Trent looked at the screen. The octopus was back, streaking towards them on jets of fire.

Arm the main guns, Benny!

The next second, he fired them.

Bolts of pure energy flickered and flashed.

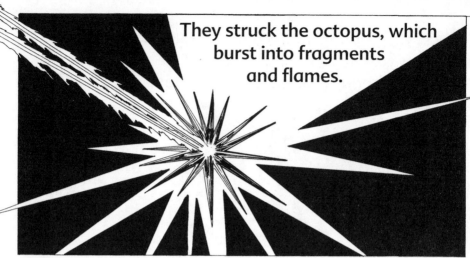
They struck the octopus, which burst into fragments and flames.

The pieces fell in a shower down to the weird planet's surface.

Sir, more creatures coming up fast!

We can't fight them all, Captain.

'Somehow,' muttered Benny, 'I don't think so.'

Trent steered Starflash closer to the surface of the metal world.

Soon it was speeding between the alien domes and towers.

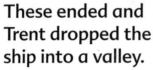
These ended and Trent dropped the ship into a valley.

Lights shone from its sloping sides, and up ahead the crew saw the looming entrance to a cave.

Do we stop or go on?

It will be a risk, whatever we do.

She pointed to the main monitor screen.

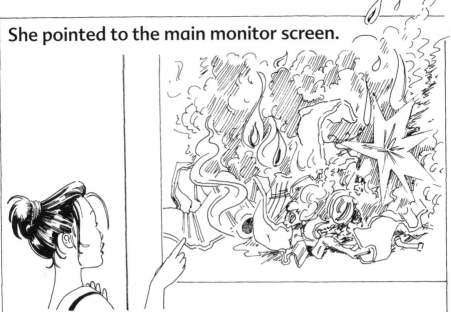

Ahead, they saw a pile of burning wreckage...
All that was left of the White Lightning.

Captain Trent made up his mind. He eased Starflash into the gloom of the cave.

Switch on all lights, Benny.

Great searchlights blazed out from the spaceship, lighting up the jagged metal walls and roof of the cave.

The floor far below was quite flat, and was marked with rows of straight lines.

Suddenly, Captain Trent understood.

This is a runway! The planet must be hollow.

But – what's inside?

Wu Li gasped.

I think I know what we're going to find.

CHAPTER SEVEN

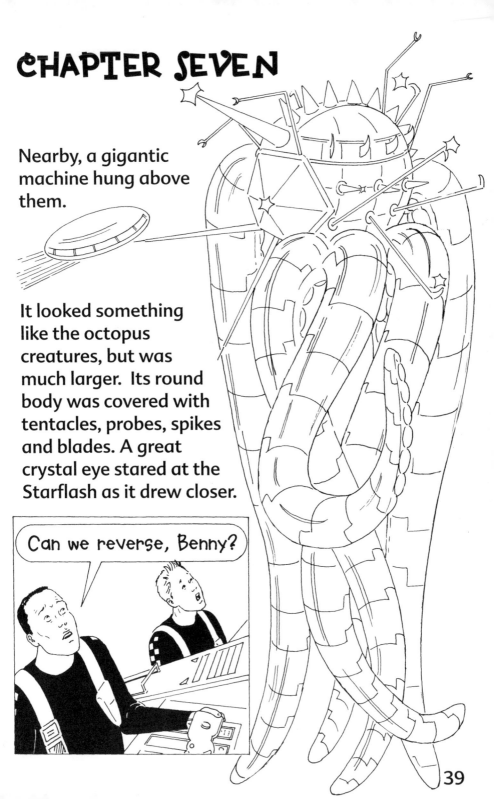

Nearby, a gigantic machine hung above them.

It looked something like the octopus creatures, but was much larger. Its round body was covered with tentacles, probes, spikes and blades. A great crystal eye stared at the Starflash as it drew closer.

Can we reverse, Benny?

But before Benny could answer, many tentacles reached out, wrapped themselves around the spaceship and began pulling it deeper into the tunnel.

oon the huge machine, with Starflash in its clutches,
rifted into a cavern that was so big, the ceiling looked
ke the sky.

Lights shone down like a hundred
suns. And on the faraway walls
hung thousands of the octopus
creatures, with many other strange
and wonderful machines.

The ship was lowered carefully to the ground.

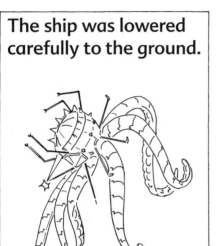

Trent took a deep breath.

Okay. Let's put our spacesuits on. We're going outside...

Five minutes later, three figures stepped out into the cavern. They wore the bright orange star uniforms of the Space Police. Trent's helmet was blue, Benny's was yellow and Wu Li's green.

Captain Trent looked at Benny's grubby headgear.

Hey, you ought to polish it when we get back.

He wanted to make his crew feel better. Benny didn't smile.

They walked away from the ship, glancing back once.

They saw the huge octopus robot hanging above Starflash, touching and probing gently with its tentacles — as though the creature meant no harm, but was simply curious.

CHAPTER EIGHT

Moving carefully, the three Space Cops reached the edge of the cavern.

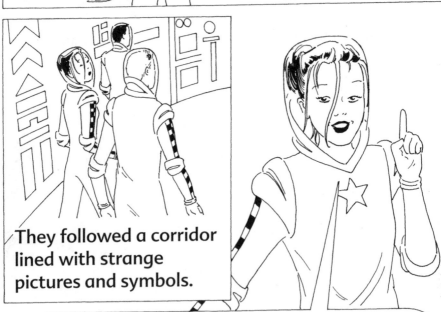

They followed a corridor lined with strange pictures and symbols.

I was right. These are the aliens that built the planet machine. They come from Ruig. They don't have any metals of their own. They're not aggressive.

Presently they came to a lift.

Well?

Nothing's harmed us so far. Let's see this through to the end.

They stepped inside. The lift sped upwards at great speed.

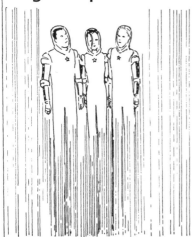

Then it stopped and the doors opened.

The Space Cops found themselves on a moving walkway, which carried them quickly to a room filled with winking lights and glowing screens.

Wu Li smiled a big smile of pure joy.

Captain, this is a computer control room!

You mean, you can understand these machines?

The girl nodded.

Yes, I think so. What's more, I know they're not hard to program. Some of them anyway.

Look.

Monitor screens... Now, if I work these controls properly...

Wu Li bent over the weird keyboards and control panels. For a time, nothing happened.

Then the screens began to blink and flicker. Pictures started to appear.

Wow! Look at that, Captain!

Some screens showed views of robots busy on the planet's surface. Elsewhere, factory chimneys poured smoke and sparks into space. Newly-made machines appeared in their hundreds.

'This world repairs itself,' Trent said quietly.

You're right.

But it must do more than that...

Wu Li was looking up.

This planet is one big machine for mining metal.

It finds a suitable place — an asteroid, or a world, and the robots begin to dig.

If a rock is too big, then it's broken up and brought back in bits!

Sounds like a useful piece of kit!

Deep space robot cameras were sending back pictures of the Asteroid Belt.

Swarms of octopuses were busy gathering them in.

The larger asteroids were being broken up into smaller pieces.

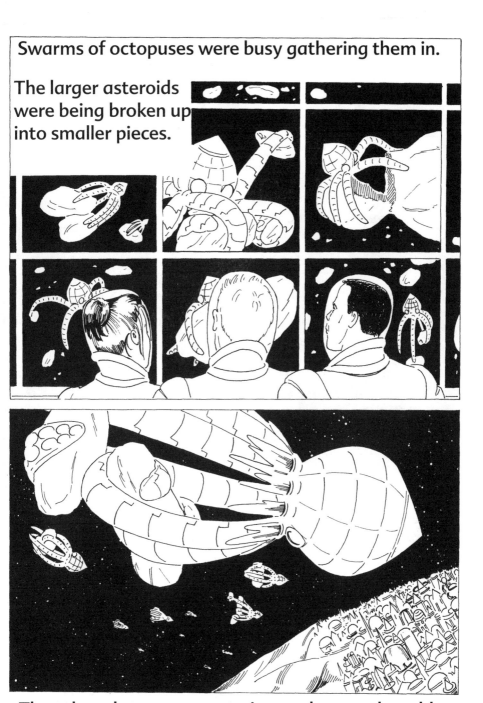

Then the robots were returning to the metal world with chunks of rock wrapped in their tentacles.

Captain Trent's face looked grim.

But don't you see, Benny. Humans didn't make this planet machine. It didn't come from Earth or Mars. But if it reaches either of those places, it's going to start mining!

Wu Li groaned suddenly.

Only if someone has managed to reprogram it.

They gazed at a new picture on the screens. It showed the planet Mars. And zooming toward it, a swarm of octopus robots.

Captain Trent clenched his teeth.

But how did the planet machine even know about Mars?

CHAPTER NINE

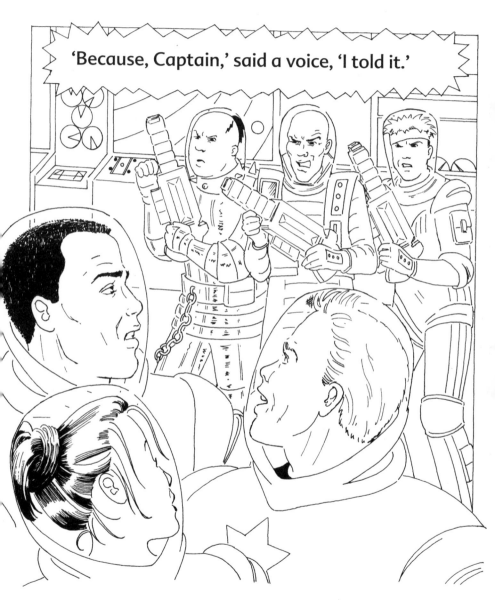

'Because, Captain,' said a voice, 'I told it.'

Trent, Benny and Wu Li spun round. Mr Sleek was standing there, Gron and Tulley by his side. All three of them held beam-guns. Mr Sleek was grinning.

And you, Captain, are just a fool!

Don't you realise what you've done?

Oh, I know exactly what I've done.
I have sent the mining robots to destroy Mars.
Once they've done that, I shall contact Earth.
I'm sure the World Government will pay any
price to keep the Earth in one piece!

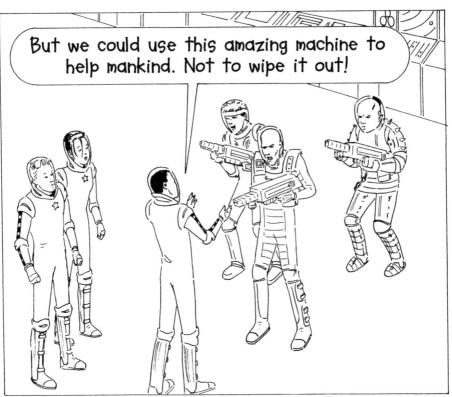

'As I said, Captain, you are a fool.' Sleek sneered.
'And now, you're going to be a dead fool also...'

He nodded to Tulley and Gron, who pointed their guns at the Space Cops.

Tulley aimed at Wu Li...

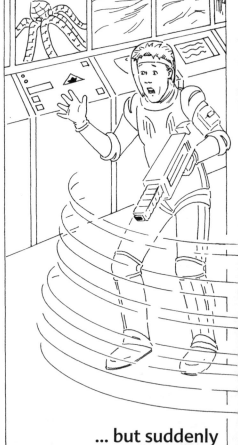

... but suddenly Wu Li was not there.

Mr Sleek started to yell a command...

... as the girl reappeared and spun close to Tulley.

A foot flashed out in a high kick and sent Tulley's beam-gun tumbling away.

Gron gave a snarl and fired at Benny.

57

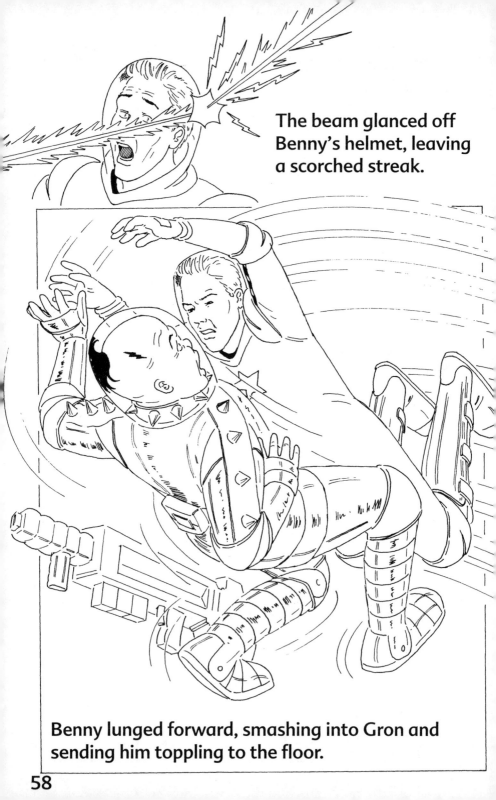

The beam glanced off Benny's helmet, leaving a scorched streak.

Benny lunged forward, smashing into Gron and sending him toppling to the floor.

Meanwhile, Mr Sleek had turned and was running for the door.

Captain Trent chased after him.

Sleek turned and fired.

Trent ducked aside as a beam of blinding energy cut through the wall.

Mr Sleek reached the door and pulled it open.

An octopus robot was hanging in the air.

It took Mr Sleek by surprise.

He yelled and lifted his gun.

The robot moved like lightning. Its tentacles wrapped around Mr Sleek's arms and body. The gun fell to the floor.

Captain Trent rushed up to Sleek, who was struggling desperately to free himself.

So you're tough and clever, eh?

Well Sleek, from now on you're also my prisoner...

CHAPTER TEN

Wu Li worked on the planet machine's computers, turning the robot swarm around in space.

They were returning home.

Mr Sleek, Gron and Tulley were safely locked up aboard the Starflash.

The three Space Cops stood beside it, looking out over the strange metal planet machine.

The question is what shall we do with it now?

We know how to reprogram it so I think we should send it back where it came from. Wu Li, would you do that for us please?

Are there any jobs I need to do before we leave, Captain?

Trent winked at Wu Li.

Yes, Benny.

This place looks a bit grubby. Maybe you'd give it a polish...